Move Fast, Act Now

A Growth Handbook

Ramesh Vemuganti

Akshay Kashyap Vemuganti

Introduction

Franklin D. Roosevelt, the longest-serving U.S. president who served more than two terms, once stated, "We cannot always build the future for our youth, but we can build our youth for the future." This sentiment highlights the importance of investing in the development and education of young people, especially given that over 30% of India's population - approximately 420 million individuals - are youth.

To ensure a bright future for our youth, we must first seek to understand the nature of the future they are facing. The future today differs fundamentally from 50 years ago, defined by an exponential growth in uncertainty. Technological advancements are rapidly accelerating, with new products and services being developed and released at unprecedented speeds, often with vastly improved performance. Many industries have now fully embraced advanced technologies like artificial intelligence (AI), creating a 'fear of missing out' mentality for both people and companies who have not yet incorporated these innovations.

Furthermore, the intensifying competition amid growing inflation has made the job market increasingly nuanced and challenging. There are valid concerns that technological progress, particularly in automation and AI, may eliminate a significant number of entry-level and middle-level jobs. This shifting landscape has forced job seekers to develop more specialized and adaptable skill sets in order to remain competitive.

To adequately prepare our youth for this dynamic and unpredictable future, we must deeply understand the complex forces shaping it. Only then can we implement educational and training programs that equip the next generation with the knowledge, skills and mindset required to navigate and thrive in the world that lies ahead.

The COVID-19 pandemic, coupled with geopolitical instability, inflation, rising interest rates, and a lack of high-quality education, has resulted in significant skill gaps, particularly among the youth. This complex scenario of economic uncertainty has set in globally. Educated and skilled youth are crucial to determining every country's future, yet a concerning gap exists between expectations and reality. Today's students and job seekers often lack the required skills and must continually unlearn, learn, and relearn to adapt to the rapidly changing market dynamics. These factors have plunged many economies into slow growth or recession.

Building and investing in high-skill jobs poses a significant challenge for larger countries like the USA, UK, Canada, and India. While governments and the public sector play key roles in providing employment opportunities for the youth, self-reliance remains the best approach. The future belongs to those who are willing to invest in themselves. People often underestimate their own potential and what they can achieve through proper preparation and planning.

This book aims to guide readers through a journey of how the youth can thrive by:

1. Inspiring them to think big
2. Crafting a game plan
3. Gaining a global perspective
4. Playing for the long run

India exemplifies this self-reliant spirit, with incredible self-made billionaires emerging from the entrepreneurial landscape. Figures like Nikhil Kamath (Founder of Zerodha), Radhakishan Damani

(Founder of D-Mart), and the co-founders of Flipkart, Sachin and Binny Bansal, showcase the passion, ferocity, and mindset of the new India. This new India is a vibrant and bold digital nation rooted in education, technology, and the arts. With over 1.2 billion mobile subscribers, including 750 million smartphones, and accelerated 5G plans, India is poised to birth new opportunities in e-commerce, media, gaming, manufacturing, and healthcare. As a mobile-first country, India leads in the early adoption of digital innovations, such as boasting the highest number of digital payment transactions globally (~100 billion and growing).

India's uniqueness sets it apart from the West, as described by Edward Luce in "In Spite of the Gods": "In the West, you have to belong to a society and follow a certain pattern. You are supposed to get a house, a career, and the whole life is oriented towards money. India is not like that. India is a unique country." India's diversity forms its strength, brand, and image, stemming from its tolerance and acceptance of foreigners. Heterogeneity in every aspect of life creates a complex social hierarchy but opens a new world of history and context. From exporting top tech talent to Bollywood's global influence, or the success of "Naatu Naatu," or Palki Sharma's leading voice in geopolitics, India offers the greatest opportunity and challenge for all generations to experience the richness of Bharat.

Ultimately, India's large and youthful population presents a massive opportunity for economic growth, but also requires strategic investment and empowerment of the next generation to harness this potential fully.

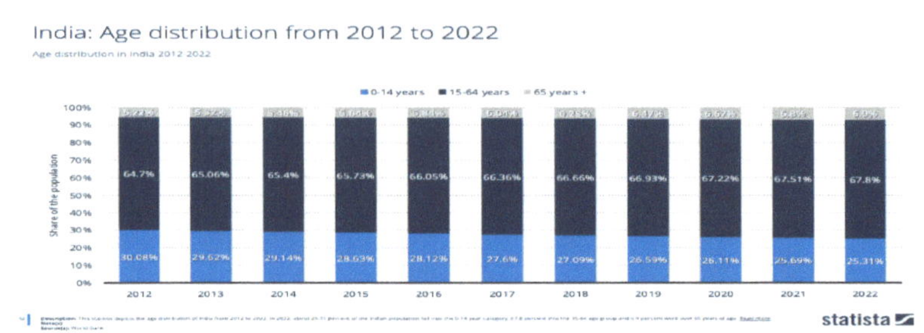

Despite the immense potential of India's youth population, the unemployment rate continues to rise sharply. This is a critical challenge that must be addressed through strategic interventions.

This book aims to equip the youth with the specific skills and mindset required to thrive in the emerging 'New India'. By providing practical guidance and insights, the book empowers young people to navigate the complex, rapidly evolving landscape and unlock their full potential.

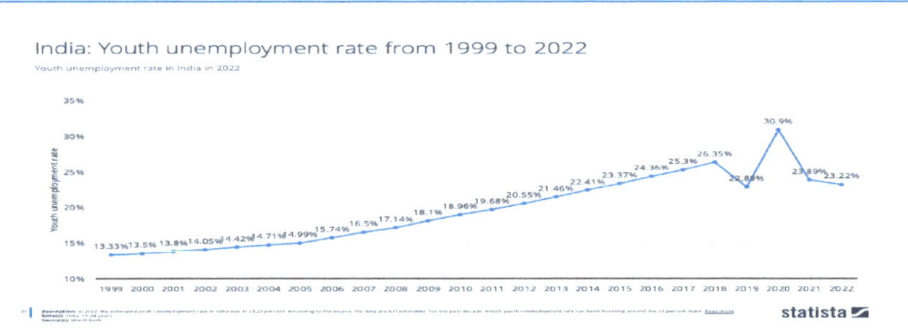

We also want to empower youth by eliminating the fear and uncertainty they may feel about the future, business, and employment opportunities. We encourage young readers to embrace two powerful mantras: 'Readers are Leaders' and 'Learners are Winners'.

By increasing their understanding of their chosen subjects, areas of specialization, market trends, industry sectors, prominent companies, and emerging technologies, youth can reduce the anxiety and trepidation they may have about the path ahead. Greater knowledge translates to greater confidence – readers succeed, and learners win.

We inspire youth to make a daily commitment to expanding their knowledge and continually sharpening their skill sets across multiple domains. This continuous learning mindset is the foundation for building unstoppable careers that can withstand the dynamic changes and challenges of the modern world.

In addition to promoting a thirst for knowledge, this book also champions the values of gratitude, kindness, and compassion. We urge young readers to be more giving, empathetic, and supportive towards their friends, families, and wider communities. By cultivating these positive traits, we can work together to make the world a safer, kinder, and more peaceful place.

Ultimately, this book provides the youth of today with the tools, strategies, and mindset shifts required to embrace the future with courage, resilience, and a commitment to bettering both themselves and the world around them

Table of Contents

Chapter 1
Heritage for growth

Humans are inherently driven by a desire for progress and the pursuit of specific life goals - whether it's landing a dream job, building a successful business, earning an advanced degree, or championing a cause. However, the boldness and scope of our aspirations are often shaped by the societal and historical context we exist within. Before embarking on our personal quests, it's valuable to reflect on India's own remarkable evolution.

Gaining independence in 1947 with a population of 300 million, India's early development was characterized by a heavy reliance on agriculture and primitive communication technologies like telegrams. Yet, under the visionary leadership of Prime Minister Jawaharlal Nehru, the country embarked on an ambitious program of industrialization and institution-building. Nehru oversaw the establishment of critical public sector undertakings, the construction of landmark infrastructure projects like the Bhakra Nangal dam, and the founding of prestigious educational institutions such as the IITs and IIMs.

Nehru's successor, Indira Gandhi, continued this developmental path, nationalizing banks, introducing social welfare schemes, and elevating the living standards of the underprivileged. However, India at this time maintained a relatively closed economy, with a traditional societal mindset where men were the primary breadwinners and women focused on domestic responsibilities.

The transformative shift began in the 1980s under Prime Minister Rajiv Gandhi, who ushered in economic liberalization and the telecom revolution. This paved the way for the explosive growth of India's IT services industry, as the country quickly adapted to emerging technologies and built capabilities across hardware, software, and systems implementation.

The economic reforms of 1991, led by Prime Minister Narasimha Rao and Finance Minister Manmohan Singh, further opened the floodgates for multinational corporations to access India's vast consumer base of 870 million people. This catalyzed a period of rapid business expansion, job creation, and the rise of a burgeoning middle class.

In the past two decades, India has continued to evolve, with the emergence of homegrown startups disrupting traditional industries and the rapid nationwide expansion of large retailers and banks. Cultural values have also shifted, with men increasingly sharing household responsibilities as women have entered the workforce in greater numbers.

This remarkable journey, from a largely agrarian economy to a globally connected, technologically advanced nation, provides valuable context for understanding the immense potential and opportunities that lie ahead for the aspirations of India's youth. By examining this transformative narrative, we can better envision and shape the bold, progressive futures we seek to create.

The visionary words of the American president resonate profoundly with India today. As the world's most populous democracy, India boasts a staggering 1.42 billion people, with 600 million aged 20 to 40 years spread across 28 states and 8 union territories. This makes India the undisputed global leader in terms of its youthful population.

Interestingly, India's vast diversity is reflected in the fact that deep cultural aspects like food, language, clothing, customs, and social systems can change dramatically every 150 miles. This remarkable heterogeneity prompts several profound questions:

1. How prepared and equipped is this vast youth population to build unstoppable, future-ready careers?
2. What unique challenges do they face while pursuing their personal and professional dreams?
3. Do they possess the iron-will, adaptability, and warrior-like mindset required to overcome these obstacles and emerge victorious?

Delving deeper into these questions reveals the complex, multifaceted challenges and deeply rooted issues facing our nation. For instance, the rural and agricultural realities of India paint a sobering picture - 60% of Indians live in villages and rural areas, 42% of the workforce depends on agriculture, and 80% are marginal and poor farmers with less than 2 acres of land.

On the digital front, the metrics are staggering - 658 million internet users, 47% internet penetration, 1.2 billion mobile subscribers, 750 million smartphones, 70 billion digital payment transactions, 17GB monthly average data per user, 5 hours of daily content consumption, and 467 million monthly social media users. These statistics give rise to critical questions:

- How can we effectively process and leverage such vast volumes of data at scale?
- What kind of infrastructure will be required to sustain this exponential digital growth?
- Are our universities and colleges equipped with high-quality faculty to build the capabilities of the next generation?
- Are Indian youth truly prepared to tackle the complex, global challenges that lie ahead?

Unraveling the answers to these multifaceted questions is crucial to understanding the true potential and preparedness of India's youth - the very foundation upon which the nation's future will be built.

Chapter 2
Problems are opportunities

This chapter explores the pressing challenges and emerging opportunities facing the youth of today, with a focus on technological, media, and healthcare-related solutions.

Drawing inspiration from the wise words of Henry Ford, who stated, "Anyone who stops learning is old. Anyone who keeps learning is young. The purpose of life is to keep the mind young," we encourage readers to reframe their approach to problem-solving. Every challenge in fact presents a new opportunity - the key is to cultivate a mindset of childlike curiosity, empathize deeply with the core issues at hand, and then construct innovative solutions.

For instance, consider the common scenario of job interview rejections due to weak coding and communication skills. The solution lies in proactively improving one's writing, reading, and coding abilities - by coding small projects, writing synopsis, and seeking feedback from seasoned software engineers. Through this iterative process of skill-building and confidence-boosting, the candidate can then confidently retry the interviews.

Solving complex, high-impact problems inevitably involve higher levels of risk, but the potential rewards can be transformative. This 'opportunity-risk' trade-off, as explored in economics, requires carefully weighing the potential losses against the benefits of pursuing one option over another.

The inspiring success stories of Indian-origin leaders heading global corporations in the United States - such as Satya Nadella at Microsoft, Sundar Pichai at Google, Arvind Krishna at IBM, Indra

Nooyi at PepsiCo, Shantanu Narayen at Adobe, and Ajay Banga at Mastercard - illustrate the power of calculated risk-taking. These individuals left their comfort zones, pursued higher education and careers abroad, navigated challenges like homesickness and cultural adaptation, and ultimately shaped remarkable careers and lives.

This universal framework of opportunity-risk can be applied to a plethora of life decisions, from professionals pursuing advanced degrees while working and raising families, to the countless untapped possibilities across various sectors. In the sections that follow, we will delve deeper into several key domains brimming with potential for the youth of India.

By embracing a mindset of continuous learning, cultivating empathy-driven problem-solving, and thoughtfully navigating the opportunity-risk paradigm, the next generation can unlock transformative outcomes for themselves and the nation.

India: Distribution of the workforce across economic sectors from 2011 to 2021

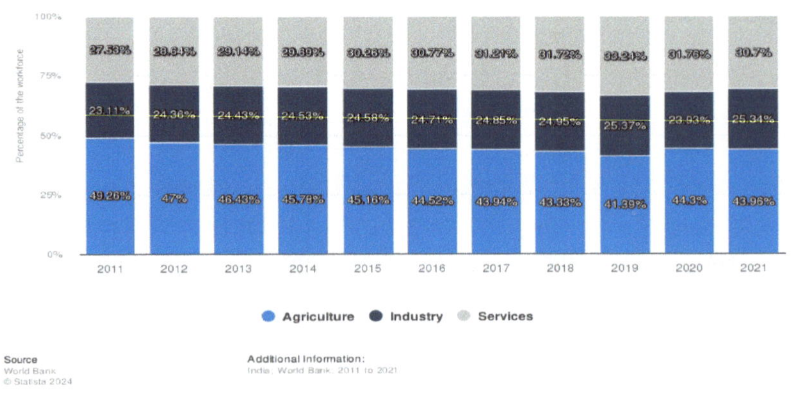

While agriculture continues to be a significant employer, accounting for 43.96% of India's workforce as of 2021, several other sectors offer massive untapped opportunities for the nation's dynamic youth.

Content Creation: India's rich history and cultural heritage provide a wellspring of storytelling potential. From grandparents sharing epic Mahabharata tales to the latest Bollywood blockbusters, narratives permeate every aspect of Indian life. With the country's population consuming over 5 hours of content daily - the world's highest - the demand for creative professionals in sectors like film, television, and digital media is immense. India's prolific movie industry, producing around 2,000 films annually across 35 languages, presents a wealth of opportunities for aspiring writers, directors, actors, and producers.

Food and Beverage: India's diverse culinary landscape, with its distinctive spices and flavors, captivates global audiences. The thriving restaurant industry, fueled by people's insatiable love for dining out and sharing their culinary experiences, offers a plethora of lifestyle and career opportunities. Beyond the food sector, the burgeoning beverage industry, particularly the spirits and wine segments, also holds promise, with specialized roles like sommeliers (wine stewards) commanding high salaries in upscale establishments.

Healthcare: While this sector requires significant investment, it serves critical needs, especially in rural India, where access to adequate acute care facilities remains a challenge. Even as urban and middle-class residents enjoy access to health insurance, the rural and below-poverty-line populations remain underserved, presenting opportunities to develop innovative healthcare solutions. Additionally, the wellness industry, encompassing gyms, yoga studios, and other fitness-related ventures, caters to the health-conscious urban demographic.

Real Estate: Home ownership continues to be a cherished status symbol in India, offering strong opportunities in building affordable, high-quality dream homes for the next generation of Indian families. Beyond construction, the rental income market provides a steady revenue stream for the middle class.

Education: As India strives to upskill its workforce at scale, opportunities abound in strengthening academic systems or creating innovative education startups to augment learning in areas like communication, science, arts, public relations, and technology. The current workforce also requires extensive upskilling in executive education and emerging technologies, while universities struggle with faculty shortages, opening doors for skilled youth to enter the teaching profession.

Tourism: In 2022, the tourism industry created 14.6 million jobs, accounting for 1 in 13 positions across India. By 2033, the sector is expected to create 58.2 million positions, and by 2024, it is projected to generate $24 billion in revenue. India's diverse geography and rich heritage offer a wide range of tourism opportunities, from Himalayan trekking to exploring architectural marvels like the Taj Mahal. Additionally, the growing medical tourism sector attracts international patients seeking premium surgical procedures.

Other promising sectors include Energy, Media, Government, Semiconductors, Manufacturing, and Automotive. Aspiring youth can leverage resources like LinkedIn, news websites, colleges, and social media to identify and explore entry points into these dynamic industries.

Ultimately, tackling the challenges in these sectors requires a deep, thorough understanding of the core issues at hand. By clearly defining the problems on paper, innovative solutions can emerge, empowering the next generation of Indian leaders to drive transformative change.

Chapter 3
Identify what you are good at

An old saying states that "a broken clock is right twice a day" - implying that no matter who you are, where you live, or what level of access you have, you possess a core skill or talent at which you inherently excel. The challenge, however, arises when many individuals fail to recognize and fully leverage these unique strengths, sometimes leading them to make suboptimal career choices.

Some people naturally excel at math, while others possess exceptional oratory skills and speak eloquently. Some individuals produce high-quality written content prolifically, while others have an exceptional emotional intelligence and interact exceptionally well with people. The key is to identify your own natural strengths.

To uncover your core competencies, we encourage you to proactively seek feedback from your friends, family members, and those you spend the most time with. Allow them to share their observations and perceptions of your unique abilities and talents. This external perspective can provide invaluable insights that you may have overlooked within yourself.

To further contextualize this exercise, LinkedIn recently published a list of the 10 most in-demand skills in the current job market. If, for instance, you identify sales as a core strength, the next logical step would be to find companies or sales managers actively seeking individuals with those capabilities.

Various avenues exist to conduct an effective job hunt, starting with leveraging the power of LinkedIn. Additionally, reach out to your network of friends and family, and even consider connecting with universities or professors who may be able to provide references and introductions within their professional networks. By proactively socializing your core skills and strengths, you may find that opportunities start coming your way.

For example, if one of your cousins is aware of a company requiring skilled product sellers, they could provide you with a valuable lead to get your foot in the door. The key is to be self-aware, actively seek feedback, and then strategically position yourself for the right opportunities that align with your natural talents.

By embracing this approach, you can unlock your true potential and embark on a fulfilling career path that capitalizes on your unique strengths and abilities.

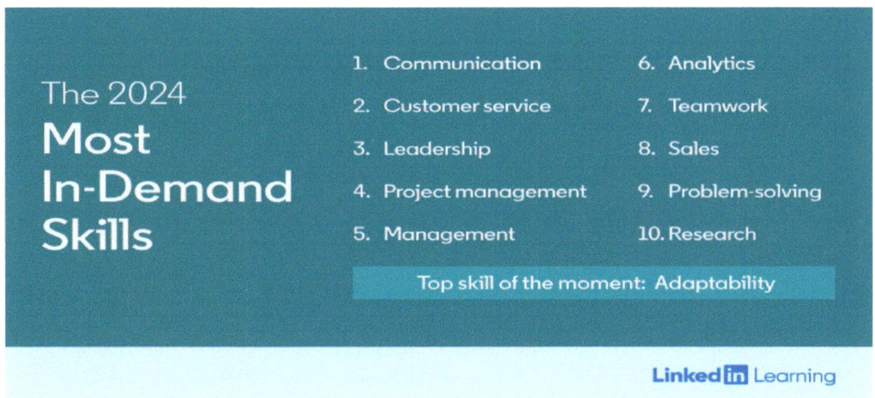

The good news is that if you have identified skill gaps or struggled to secure a job, this signals an opportunity to revisit the drawing board and actively learn new skills. Thanks to the information explosion of the internet age over the past 20 years, you can now self-teach most new competencies or acquire them through self-directed passion and interest.

This shift towards a knowledge economy and technology revolution has produced an inundation of information, knowledge, and emerging technologies across all domains. Those who embrace this wave of learning stand to benefit the most.

While seasoned leaders and executives possess valuable contemporary management knowledge and industry expertise to guide institutions, companies, and universities, the academic landscape is often plagued by an overdose of theoretical content without adequate real-world startup or industry experience. To propel India into a phase of hyper-growth, this paradigm must evolve.

More industry professionals should be encouraged to participate in guest lectures and serve in part-time academic roles to help bridge the gap between theory and practice. This mutually beneficial 'flywheel' will drive higher-quality research, knowledge exchange, and ultimately raise the overall standards of education in the nation.

The key is to cultivate an insatiable curiosity and maintain a lifelong learning mindset. The more you learn, the more opportunities will come your way, and the better you can market your evolving skill set. Upskilling in high-demand domains like Generative AI, Data Analytics, and Cloud Computing, combined with the development of essential generalist capabilities in product development, marketing, sales, and operations, can significantly enhance your employability.

Drawing inspiration from the Mahabharata, when the great warrior Bhishma shared his vast knowledge with the Pandavas before departing this world, we must recognize the fleeting nature of such repositories of wisdom. Similarly, in today's rapidly changing landscape, we must proactively seek out and learn from industry veterans and thought leaders before their expertise is lost.

As the famous comedian Mel Brooks aptly said, "If you're quiet, you're not living. You've got to be noisy and colorful and lively." Beyond technical skills, developing soft skills like networking, interpersonal communication, time management, problem-solving, leadership, and empathy are equally crucial. Management, as both a science and an art, is underpinned by the accumulated wisdom of profound thinkers like Frederick Taylor, Henri Fayol, and the legendary Peter Drucker, the father of modern management.

Finally, once you have identified your strengths and feel confident in your abilities, you must maintain a relentless, continuous effort. Keep applying, networking, and leave no stone unturned. Embrace feedback, course-correct when necessary, and never let a "no" deter you from pursuing your aspirations.

Chapter 4
Understand the deep tech revolution

When computers first entered the world, many believed they would only be used for basic data processing and accounting tasks, merely eliminating the drudgery of manual labor. However, the remarkable evolution of technology over the past 80 years, driven by exponential advancements in chip processing power and software development, has given birth to transformative tools like ChatGPT in 2023. Today, the applications of this technological progress span a wide spectrum, from the diagnosis of serious ailments in healthcare to advancements in governance, consumer behavior analysis, virtual reality, the use of drones in agriculture and manufacturing, and beyond.

As one insightful author noted, "We are moving from a world of problems, which demand speed, analysis, and the elimination of uncertainty to solve, to a world of dilemmas, which demand patience, sense-making, and an engagement with uncertainty." It is within this context that the rise of Artificial Intelligence (AI) proves particularly intriguing.

At its core, AI refers to the development of computer systems that can perform tasks typically requiring human intelligence, such as learning, problem-solving, decision-making, perception, and language processing. This involves creating algorithms and models that can analyze data, recognize patterns, and make predictions or decisions based on that analysis - essentially mimicking aspects of human cognition, including reasoning, learning, and adaptation.

Several distinct approaches to AI exist, including Machine Learning (training algorithms on large datasets to identify patterns and make predictions), Deep Learning (a subset of machine learning that uses artificial neural networks inspired by the human brain), Natural Language Processing (techniques enabling computers to understand, interpret, and generate human language), Computer Vision (algorithms that can identify and process objects, scenes, and activities in images and videos), and Expert Systems (AI systems using a knowledge base of rules and information to solve complex problems within specific domains).

The applications of AI span a wide range of industries, from healthcare and finance to transportation, manufacturing, and entertainment. It can perform tasks such as image and speech recognition, language translation, recommendation systems, predictive analytics, and the automation of repetitive processes.

While AI has undoubtedly made significant advancements, challenges and limitations remain, including the need for large amounts of high-quality data, the potential for biases in data or algorithms, and the difficulty of achieving general intelligence comparable to humans across a broad range of tasks. Additionally, AI development raises critical ethical concerns related to privacy, security, accountability, and the potential impact on employment and society as a whole, which require careful consideration and addressing.

According to experts, AI can confer a significant technological advantage to products and services, and is often considered a core competency of businesses or even individual entrepreneurs. This core competence can prove to be a reliable asset during economic downturns, recessions, and slowdowns, as even sluggish economies can find solutions by applying AI to business and entrepreneurship.

In the context of India, given the sheer scale of the nation's population and resources, the opportunities presented by the strategic and widespread application of AI are immense. By effectively leveraging and understanding this transformative technology, India can nurture wealth creation and significantly improve the living standards of its citizens. As the global landscape shifts, with countries now competing on the basis of technology and innovation rather than economic models alone, AI represents the tip of the iceberg - a vital core competency that can elevate the nation's development trajectory.

The United States rise as a global superpower can be largely attributed to its thriving culture of technological entrepreneurship. As more nations seek to emulate this model, India stands poised to harness its immense potential and blossom across diverse sectors.

The traditional textbook definition of the Knowledge Economy, comprising four key pillars, provides a useful framework to consider how transformative technologies like Artificial Intelligence (AI) can be strategically applied. Let's explore a couple of critical industries - education and healthcare - where AI holds the promise of driving meaningful impact.

Q1: How can AI help improve the Indian education system?

AI can enhance the Indian education landscape in several compelling ways:

1. Personalized Learning: AI-powered adaptive learning systems can analyze a student's strengths, weaknesses, learning pace, and preferences to deliver personalized learning experiences, optimizing the process for individual needs.
2. Intelligent Tutoring Systems: AI-based tutoring applications can provide real-time feedback, identify knowledge gaps, and offer customized learning materials and exercises, essentially acting as virtual tutors that complement traditional classroom teaching.
3. Language Learning: In a multilingual country like India, AI-powered language learning apps can offer personalized instruction, speech recognition, and feedback on pronunciation and grammar, significantly aiding the acquisition of new languages.
4. Automated Grading and Assessment: AI algorithms can automate the grading of assignments, essays, and tests, reducing the workload on teachers while providing faster feedback to students. Additionally, AI can design adaptive assessments tailored to each student's level.
5. Educational Content Generation: AI can generate a wide range of educational content, such as practice questions, explanations, and learning materials, based on specific

topics or concepts, helping create customized resources at scale.

6. Student Engagement and Motivation: AI-powered virtual assistants and chatbots can interact with students, answer queries, and provide guidance and motivation, keeping them engaged and interested in their learning journey.
7. Administrative Tasks Automation: AI can automate various administrative tasks in educational institutions, such as student enrollment, attendance tracking, timetable scheduling, and record-keeping, improving efficiency and reducing the workload on administrative staff.
8. Learning Analytics: AI can analyze data from sources like student performance, attendance, and engagement to provide insights into learning patterns and identify areas for improvement, empowering educators to make data-driven decisions.
9. Educational Resource Recommendation: AI algorithms can recommend relevant educational resources, such as books, videos, or online courses, based on a student's interests, learning style, and academic performance.
10. Accessibility and Inclusivity: AI-powered assistive technologies, including text-to-speech and speech-to-text tools, can help make education more accessible for students with disabilities, promoting greater inclusivity.

While implementing AI in Indian education may face infrastructure limitations, data privacy concerns, and the need for teacher training, addressing these challenges can unlock the transformative potential of this technology to enhance the country's education system.

Q2: How can AI improve the lives of people in India?

AI can play a significant role in enhancing healthcare in India by addressing key challenges and improving the quality and accessibility of services:

1. Disease Diagnosis and Prediction: AI algorithms can analyze medical images and patient data to assist in accurate diagnosis and early detection of diseases, while predictive models can identify high-risk individuals for preventive measures.
2. Drug Discovery and Development: AI can accelerate the drug discovery process by simulating molecular interactions and identifying potential candidates efficiently. It can also optimize clinical trials and analyze large trial data for faster, more cost-effective drug development.
3. Remote Patient Monitoring: AI-powered wearables and mobile apps can monitor vital signs, symptoms, and treatment adherence, enabling remote monitoring and timely interventions, thereby improving healthcare access in underserved areas.
4. Virtual Healthcare Assistants: AI chatbots and virtual assistants can provide basic medical advice, triage patients, schedule appointments, monitor chronic conditions, and give medication reminders, enhancing access to primary care and improving disease management.
5. Healthcare Resource Optimization: AI can optimize the allocation of hospital beds, equipment, and staff by predicting demand and identifying bottlenecks, ensuring efficient resource utilization and improved patient care.
6. Medical Research and Clinical Decision Support: AI can analyze large medical research datasets, identify patterns, and generate insights to advance scientific knowledge. Clinical decision support systems can provide real-time

recommendations, improving diagnostic accuracy and treatment planning.

7. Fraud Detection and Claim Processing: AI algorithms can detect fraudulent insurance claims and billing, reducing costs and ensuring proper resource allocation. Automated claim processing can also streamline reimbursement, reducing administrative burdens.
8. Mental Health Support: AI chatbots and virtual assistants can provide mental health support, counseling, and guidance, addressing the shortage of mental health professionals in India and encouraging more people to seek help through anonymity and accessibility.

While implementing AI in Indian healthcare requires addressing data quality, privacy, and ethical concerns, its potential to improve accessibility, affordability, and quality is significant. Collaborative efforts between healthcare providers, researchers, and technology companies will be crucial in realizing the full benefits of AI for the Indian healthcare system.

Chapter 5
Move Fast, Act Now

The short answer is that there are no shortcuts to success in life. You must play it right and move strategically. As an ice hockey legend once famously said, one must "skate to where the puck is going, not where it went." This metaphor eloquently emphasizes the importance of anticipation, vision, and forward-thinking to achieve success.

In hockey, the puck moves incredibly fast, and skilled players don't just react to its present position. Instead, they anticipate where the puck is going and position themselves accordingly. This requires a deep understanding of the game, the ability to read patterns and trajectories, and the capacity to make decisions based on where the play is heading.

The same principle applies to various aspects of life, including business, career, and personal growth:

Anticipate Trends: Successful individuals and organizations anticipate future trends and position themselves accordingly. By studying market patterns, consumer behavior, and emerging technologies, they identify opportunities before others and gain a competitive advantage.

Adopt a Forward-Thinking Mindset: Instead of merely reacting and staying stuck in the present, a forward-thinking mindset allows you to proactively shape your future. This involves setting long-term goals, developing strategies, and making decisions that align with where you want to be.

Adapt and Be Agile: Those who adapt quickly and pivot their approach are more likely to succeed in a constantly changing world. By anticipating change and being agile, you can stay ahead of the curve and capitalize on new opportunities.

Strategic Positioning: Just like hockey players positioning themselves for where the puck is going, individuals and organizations can strategically position themselves for future success. This may involve acquiring new skills, building strategic partnerships, or entering new markets before others.

Continuous Learning and Improvement: To effectively anticipate and adapt, embrace continuous learning and improvement. By staying curious, seeking knowledge, and refining skills, you can better understand where the metaphorical puck is going and position yourself accordingly.

The quote encourages a proactive, forward-thinking approach to life and business. By anticipating future trends and opportunities, adapting to change, and positioning yourself strategically, you increase your chances of success and stay ahead of the curve.

Ultimately, the key is to approach life and your goals with a positive, growth-oriented mindset. Cultivate self-belief, develop patience and tolerance, and consistently work on improving your strengths and addressing your weaknesses. When you do so, you unlock your true potential and pave the way for sustainable success and fulfillment.

Also, the COVID-19 pandemic has undoubtedly led many individuals to adopt more sedentary lifestyles. However, the key to getting active again lies in finding meaning and purpose in one's work. Seeking meaningful "work" is an art in itself, requiring effort to approach others, have thoughtful conversations, and offer valuable skills to deliver and contribute.

Over time, this initial part-time "work" can evolve into a full-time job. It's a cyclical process - today we seek, tomorrow someone seeks us, and we pay it forward. The act of creating, discussing, and evaluating work is the best way to stay engaged and keep moving forward.

Building on one's strengths is crucial, and continuous improvement coupled with competing with oneself are the most powerful traits. This journey begins by identifying one's growth areas and addressing them proactively. For some, it may be weight management, for others, financial management or career advancement, and for some, it could be maintaining a job or navigating a tough personal/family struggle.

Here are examples of how weaknesses can become growth areas and ultimately strengths:

1. Laziness and lethargy: Surround yourself with active, high-energy friends to accomplish tasks during the day.
2. Struggling with goals: Set a few achievable goals (e.g., 15 minutes of workout, 30 minutes of writing, saving 1000 INR this month) and strive to achieve them.

3. Inhibition to ask questions: Overcome shyness in social settings and at work by asking curious questions, which can lead to new opportunities.
4. Dealing with the unknown: While it's impossible to become an expert in every topic, choose a few areas to deepen your knowledge and skills.
5. Anger management: Release endorphins through yoga, breathing exercises, and workouts to reduce and control anger.
6. Intolerance: Tactfully tolerate others in life to sustain relationships, while avoiding abuse.
7. Impatience: Develop patience, when necessary, as not every situation requires an instant reaction or response.
8. Global exposure: Expand your horizons by using the internet, friends, and family to inquire about world events and identify ways to benefit or leverage them.
9. Lacking empathy: Cultivate the ability to genuinely care about others and resonate with their feelings, a powerful trait.
10. Device addiction: Maintain a healthy balance, and whenever possible, opt for voice conversations over texting with loved ones.
11. Negative energy: Instead of sharing negative thoughts, release them through workouts, chatting with friends, or taking a stroll.

It's important to note that not all these problems can be solved overnight. Leaders must understand this and create opportunities for people to take advantage across the board, especially when in a position to make an impact.

A major source of distress and mental anxiety in Indian families and society is the tendency to compare oneself with siblings, classmates, cousins, colleagues, in-laws, and neighbors. This comparison-driven mindset is the root cause of disgruntlement and loss of balance. Everyone is on their own journey, and it's crucial to appreciate what you have, be happy with it, and work towards what you desire. Comparison often leads to an undesirable inferiority complex, and it's better to genuinely enjoy others' success.

The powerful Karma philosophy applies here - "What goes around comes around." It's okay not to be okay, as everyone has their own time. Ups and downs are a natural part of life, and every problem has a time limit. During tough times, one must remain strong, sincere to their profession, work hard, respect loved ones, and help others whenever possible. By embodying these positive traits, one can ultimately achieve happiness and fulfillment.

Chapter 6
Build your circle of trust

Whom do you call when you have a life emergency?

Whom do you call to take care of your family when you must go away?

Whom do you call when in a low mood?

This is what we refer to as your Circle of Trust (COT) - the authentic personal, professional, and social connections that you can rely on and cultivate over a lifetime.

Building genuine, lasting relationships that span generations is invaluable, but it's important to remember that we cannot fake these bonds. True connections take time, often years, to develop and deepen. Even with our busy lives, it's crucial that we do not ignore those who have helped us in the past. Giving back, whether in the form of money, time, or resources, is essential for strengthening these lifelong relationships.

For those with families, maximizing quality time with loved ones is paramount. As the saying goes, "you've only got 18 summers with your kids" - make the most of them. Something as simple as a home-cooked family dinner can create cherished memories that last a lifetime. After all, what good are material possessions without the warmth of human connection?

As we enter the digital age, a new challenge arises for those transitioning into retirement or the next phase of life. The key is to maintain a structured daily routine that incorporates a variety of enriching activities:

- Staying informed through reading newspapers and consuming high-quality content

- Immersing yourself in favorite books, authors, and TV shows

- Engaging in regular exercise and fitness routines

- Connecting with family, friends, and extended networks

- Offering mentorship or coaching to others

- Pursuing spiritual or religious activities

- Exploring new hobbies like farming, gardening, or creative pursuits

- Continuously learning new skills, languages, or technologies

- Sharing knowledge and insights with younger generations

- Contributing to society through philanthropy or volunteering

The most valuable quality to cultivate is acceptance - the willingness to acknowledge one's own limitations, weaknesses, and areas for improvement, and then take proactive steps to address them. By embracing this mindset, seniors can find fulfillment and purpose in the next phase of their lives.

Equally important is the need to avoid comparison and embrace happiness as a choice. Sharing time, resources, and knowledge with those in need can be deeply rewarding and help overcome loneliness, which has become a universal problem.

Ultimately, the key to a fulfilling retirement or later life lies in maintaining a positive, proactive, and generous mindset. By staying engaged, continuously learning, and giving back to one's community, seniors can make a lasting impact and find deep personal satisfaction.

It is our dharmic duty that once we are in a comfortable position, we must take care of others in need. Continuous effort and constant self-improvement can lead to massive positive changes. It's important to recognize that everyone has weaknesses and blind spots. Retirement can be an ideal time to work on addressing these areas while keeping one's ego in check.

Donations are a wonderful way to support causes that align with one's passions and interests, providing a deep sense of fulfillment. Allocating 3-5% of one's salary towards charitable causes or helping those in need can make a meaningful impact.

Connecting our children with their peers, grandparents, cousins, and through organized playdates and social activities holds immense value. It helps build their confidence, fosters a sense of community, and shapes well-rounded personalities, preparing them for the diverse people and situations they will encounter in life.

With increasing diaspora, it has become more challenging to stay connected with family members living out of town or abroad. It is crucial to make extra efforts to reconnect with these distant family members, letting go of any old grudges along the way. People who lose touch with their family tend to develop a negative mindset, while maintaining ties with extended family and childhood friends can be particularly meaningful, especially for those who provided support during difficult times.

Failing to stay in touch with others goes against the principles of Sanatana Dharma. A simple phone call or message can greatly enrich someone's day. Sharing our time and resources can bring us immense joy, not just personal enjoyment. The easiest way to make a positive impact is to connect those in need with resources, such as helping a friend find employment.

This process of expanding one's community can also be a source of great happiness and fulfillment. Loneliness can be a painful experience, and embracing inclusivity is essential.

Developing hobbies and interests is another valuable way to find stress relief and maintain good health. Exploring new subjects, learning foreign languages, pursuing creative outlets like music, dance, or art, engaging in sports and fitness activities, or experimenting with gardening, photography, or social media can all be immensely rewarding.

These habits not only divert the mind from negative influences and boredom but also contribute to building a more well-rounded and valuable personality.

The message is clear: push yourself today for a wonderful tomorrow. While social media can be a distraction if misused, controlling device time can greatly benefit one's ability to focus on more meaningful pursuits.

As the Hindi proverb says, "Kaal Kare So Aaj Kar, Aaj Kare So Ub Pal Mein Pralaya Hoyegi, Bahuri Karoge Kub" - meaning, "Tomorrow's work today, today's work now. If the moment is lost, how will the work be done?"

Embracing the power of the present, a five-step process can be followed to learn new skills effectively:

1. Decide what to learn
2. Research and seek advice on where to learn
3. Enroll in the course, program, or self-learn
4. Approach the learning with enthusiasm and immersion

5. Recognize that it takes 21 days to build a habit, which then becomes effortless.

Assess your progress every 90 days and repeat the cycle until you reach mastery, then move on to the next skill. The key is to avoid regrets and keep moving forward.

Setbacks and mistakes are a natural part of life, and it's important not to take them personally. As the saying goes, "even an elephant can slip." A brief analysis to understand what went wrong is fine, but dwelling on it for too long is counterproductive. Life is meant to be enjoyed, not laced with regrets.

Building a valuable, well-rounded personality takes time and effort, but it is a worthy pursuit. Not everyone is a natural social butterfly, and introverts have their own strengths. However, if one desires a full, enriching social life, it is crucial to cultivate an interesting personality.

As we age, it becomes increasingly important to be friendly and open with others to maintain a strong social circle. Making new friends and building a community can be more challenging, but it is crucial to invest the time and effort. Approach new connections without any preconceptions or hang-ups, and simply be yourself. This investment in relationships will pay dividends in the long run.

Loneliness is a universal problem today, often stemming from a lack of time spent developing meaningful connections. We may continue to read, learn, and absorb new hobbies, books, news, and online content, but there comes a point where we need to shift our focus to expressing, sharing, and disseminating our knowledge and experiences. To do this effectively, we need to surround ourselves with the right people.

Companionship does not come for free in this world - it must be earned through our efforts. Small gestures like hosting family dinners or having neighbors over for evening tea can be powerful ways to overcome loneliness. However, this is a two-way street - we must also make the effort to visit and engage with our social circle.

The COVID-19 pandemic has had a profound impact, damaging many jobs and livelihoods. As we enter the era of Generative AI and other emerging technologies, a new mental model for growth is required. Key questions arise, such as:

1. What is the way forward for Indian students and youth?
2. How should they prepare and learn to become industry-ready in an ever-changing environment?
3. How can they secure employment in the post-COVID, competitive, digital age?
4. What are the core market needs?

Empowering India's youth can yield remarkable results, as they possess valuable qualities like honesty, transparency, trustworthiness, and commitment - traits that are crucial in their daily work, jobs, and social activities. The social and economic conditions prevalent in rural India have also shaped these characteristics in the region's youth.

However, several systemic challenges impact Tier-2/3 students and youth, which must be addressed:

1. Fear of the English language in terms of speaking, reading, and listening skills. This fear needs to be alleviated, and they must understand that it is acceptable to have conversational English proficiency.
2. An inborn shyness in expressing ideas, thoughts, and needs. The social structure in villages has led to certain sections

remaining subdued and unable to voice their grievances. This must be addressed to enable all voices to be heard.

3. An age-old obsession with government jobs, leading to the careers and futures of thousands of youths being derailed. They have the misconception that there is no security in other jobs, which is no longer true. This calls for a strong, value-based education that emphasizes the importance of work over the nature or type of job.
4. Low attendance in online classes during the COVID-19 lockdown, with students offering various excuses like power issues, poor internet, lack of devices, and so on. This highlights the need for better infrastructure and access to technology.
5. Lack of curiosity and zeal for continuous learning, resulting in low knowledge levels pertaining to their subjects, the economy, market, research, and emerging technologies. Industry experts should regularly train teachers and emphasize ethics and morals in both in-person and online classrooms.
6. Narrow mindsets, where students with specific educational backgrounds only look for jobs within their domain, failing to explore the broader job market. Networking and interactions between industry professionals and students are crucial to expand their horizons.

Addressing these challenges and deficiencies requires a strategic, structured approach, involving policymakers, industry representatives, and academic institutions. The pandemic has also created unique opportunities that must be leveraged.

The key to progress lies in a change in attitude, where the youth take responsibility for their futures. This begins with establishing a daily routine and a powerful morning regimen, including exercise, abstaining from unhealthy habits, and continuous learning.

Achieving daily, weekly, monthly, and annual goals through this structured approach can lead to meaningful progress in personal, social, and professional domains.

Ultimately, the power of a daily schedule cannot be overstated. It enables individuals to make steady progress, stay focused, and maintain a positive, solution-oriented mindset, even in the face of life's challenges.

Succeeding in one's personal, social, and professional lives is crucial for a truly fulfilling existence. Along the way, there will be some hard knocks and challenges that can prove useful in both our personal and professional journeys. Sometimes, these difficulties arise naturally, while at other times, we must put in deliberate effort to overcome them. The key is to never give up. Many people erroneously expect everything to happen favorably and tend to give up too easily.

By adopting a "flow" philosophy of staying focused yet happy as a way of life, we can significantly reduce the stress in our system. Whatever obstacles we face today - be it issues with our children's education, personal relationships, dealing with customers, bosses, bankers, investors, in-laws, health concerns, career challenges, financial crunches, or conflicts with colleagues - the key is to maintain a positive, mentally strong approach.

This leads us to the importance of acceptance, which is a deep and multifaceted topic. For major life decisions, it is crucial to follow your heart and intuition. Competence builds confidence, and confidence helps eliminate excessive worrying, fear, and self-doubt. Cultivating a positive attitude, where you "think, be, and do," can lead to immense success.

Achieving daily goals and consistently delivering on your duties while working hard, without obsessing over the results, are also essential. Five crucial elements to keep achieving your objectives are:

1. Hard work and sincerity in everything you do
2. Seeking help when required, without hesitation
3. Building skills, be they academic, athletic, or creative
4. Giving back to your friends and family, and helping others
5. Embracing the powerful motto of Theodore Roosevelt: "Do what you can, with what you have, where you are"

The concept of "work is worship" and investing in self-reliance applies to all strata of society. We must educate and empower people, especially the underprivileged, on the importance of being self-reliant and not solely dependent on the government.

Effective time management is a crucial tool for "getting things done" during the day and avoiding harmful addictions like devices, alcohol, sugar, or gambling. It is said that it takes just 21 days to build powerful, transformative habits, such as learning new skills and improving one's health.

India's post-independence education policies have placed a strong emphasis on science, technology, and innovation, reflecting in the teaching, learning, and outreach processes. This unique focus on the "Science > Technology > Innovation" progression is a key strength. Communities must continue to make a difference for our nation, addressing critical gaps in areas like girls' education, access to clean water and sanitation, affordable healthcare, and housing for the urban poor.

One can pursue a multitude of activities and passions in parallel, without hindrance, and observe the positive impact they have created over time. As the famous American poet Robert Frost eloquently wrote, "The woods are lovely, dark & deep. But I have promises to keep. And miles to go before I sleep. And miles to go before I sleep" - a sentiment that resonates profoundly.

India has indeed made remarkable progress in the past 74 years, overcoming significant challenges like severe poverty, malnutrition, population growth, low-quality education, limited industry, and technological backwardness. However, new challenges now face our society, such as the need to address overpopulated cities, preserve the environment, ensure pollution-free air and clean drinking water, promote sanitation and hygiene as a way of life, and adopt sustainability as a collective motto.

The journey ahead requires us to be ready and equipped to tackle these evolving complexities with a determined, collaborative, and progressive mindset.

Chapter 7
Invest in health and happiness

The pandemic has had a profound impact on global mental health, with depression levels and social isolation on the rise, threatening overall human happiness and productivity. A recent study published in The Lancet shows that in 2022, more than 1 billion people worldwide are living with obesity. This paints a concerning picture - despite the many exciting developments happening around the world, life has become monotonous and dull for a significant portion of the population. This raises an important question: How can we effectively address these challenges?

Improving both mental health and physical well-being is crucial for enhancing the overall quality of life. Here are some effective strategies to address these aspects:

Mental Health:

- Practice mindfulness and meditation: Techniques like deep breathing, mindfulness meditation, and yoga can reduce stress, improve focus, and promote a sense of calm. Seek guidance from experienced Indian experts.

- Exercise regularly: Regular physical activity releases endorphins, which can boost mood and alleviate depression and anxiety symptoms. Simple activities like running, yoga, or bodyweight exercises can be highly beneficial.

- Get enough sleep: Aim for 7-9 hours of quality sleep each night, as sleep deprivation can negatively impact mental health. One quick tip is to establish an early bedtime routine.

- Seek social support: Build and maintain strong social connections with your close circle (friends, family, etc.), as social isolation can exacerbate mental health issues. Organize regular gatherings and attend family functions.

- Practice gratitude: Cultivate a habit of expressing gratitude, as it can shift your focus towards the positive aspects of life and improve overall well-being. Maintaining a gratitude journal can have a profound impact.

- Consider professional help: If you're struggling with persistent mental health concerns, don't hesitate to seek assistance from a mental health professional, such as a therapist or counselor. Seeking help is a sign of strength, not weakness.

Physical Health:

- Maintain a balanced diet: Eat a variety of nutrient-rich foods, including fruits, vegetables, whole grains, lean proteins, and healthy fats. Avoid excessively prioritizing any single macronutrient.

- Stay hydrated: Drink plenty of water throughout the day to support bodily functions and maintain energy levels.

- Incorporate strength training: Engage in resistance exercises, such as weight lifting or bodyweight exercises, to build muscle strength and improve bone density.

- Practice flexibility and mobility: Incorporate stretching and mobility exercises, including yoga, to maintain flexibility and reduce injury risk.

- Prioritize rest and recovery: Allow your body adequate recovery time from physical activities by incorporating rest days and getting enough sleep.

- Manage stress: Chronic stress can negatively impact physical health. Practice stress management techniques like meditation, deep breathing, or engaging in enjoyable hobbies.

- Seek professional guidance: If you have specific health concerns or want personalized advice, consult a healthcare professional, such as a doctor, nutritionist, or personal trainer.

Remember, improving mental and physical health is an ongoing process that does not happen overnight. Small, consistent steps can lead to significant positive changes over time. Be patient and persistent in your efforts.

However, improving the body and mind alone is not the complete solution. It is also crucial to focus on personal growth, discovering one's true potential, and finding contentment.

How can one achieve this? By engaging in activities that bring happiness and regularly challenging one's mind. This could involve reading high-quality content, watching informative media, pursuing education, spending quality time with family, or exploring various passions and creative pursuits.

At the same time, it is essential to avoid developing a complex or obsession with the progress of others. Everyone has their own journey, and their "time will come" with hard work and dedication.

Surround yourself with optimistic and positive people, and continuously seek to acquire new skills and knowledge. Engage in productive conversations, and participate in activities that release endorphins, the "happy hormones."

Ultimately, the key is to maintain a balanced and synergistic approach, as emphasized in the "7 Habits of Highly Effective People" by Dr. Steven Covey. Embrace proactivity, strategic thinking, prioritization, collaboration, and a commitment to self-improvement. This holistic approach can unlock the path to true happiness, fulfillment, and personal growth.

Chapter 8
Money follows the story

"You can't sell anything if you can't tell anything" - Zig Ziglar

This insightful statement underscores a fundamental truth - regardless of whether we acknowledge it or not, the reality is that we all engage in some form of selling in our daily lives. Sales is not just a profession, but a critical skill that permeates various aspects of our personal and professional lives.

Contrary to the common misconception, sales is a versatile discipline, on par with other core business functions like product development, finance, human resources, and research & development. There are thousands of sales roles across industries, from startups to large enterprises, including in sectors like education and healthcare. However, many young professionals and students remain unaware of the immense opportunities in this field.

The truth is, effective sales require a combination of product knowledge, communication skills, negotiation capabilities, and a deep understanding of customer needs and motivations. It is not merely about "chasing" people and making pitches, as often depicted. Sales is a formal organizational discipline that takes years to master.

Whether you want to convince a friend to join you on a trip, persuade your spouse to see a movie, impress a hiring manager to land a job, or get your parents' approval for a relationship - in all these instances, you must effectively sell your proposition. Sales and closing skills are foundational to success in interviews, pitching startup ideas to investors, and securing new projects or promotions.

Yet, the irony is that not many universities and colleges provide comprehensive sales education. While significant resources are dedicated to product development, technology, engineering, and design, the sales function is often overlooked. The reality is that most sales expertise comes not from textbook knowledge, but from real-world experience and learning from others.

Sales is a process, a philosophy, and a scientific body of knowledge with proven methods and techniques that bring new customers to an organization. It is the lifeblood that sustains businesses, as the old adage goes - "Sales fixes everything." Just like other critical business functions, sales are a core competency that must be nurtured and developed.

To get started, it's essential to understand the fundamental differences between sales and marketing. While marketing focuses on promoting, negotiating, and facilitating the exchange of goods or services, sales involve a series of activities aimed at identifying potential customers, understanding their needs, presenting solutions, and ultimately persuading them to make a purchase.

The key steps in the sales process include prospecting, qualifying, pre-approach, approach, presentation, overcoming objections, closing, and follow-up. Mastering these elements, along with developing effective communication, negotiation, and customer relationship skills, is crucial for sales success.

Contrary to the common misconception, great sales professionals are not merely "liars" or "deceivers." Truly effective sales require a deep understanding of the consumer mindset, pain points, and the right strategies to address them. This could involve leveraging word-of-mouth marketing in certain contexts, rather than relying solely on traditional advertising.

Ultimately, sales, marketing, and storytelling are inextricably linked and play a vital role in the success of any business or organization. By combining these elements, companies can build strong customer connections, differentiate themselves from competitors, and drive sustainable growth.

The power of storytelling in sales and marketing cannot be overstated, as it allows for emotional connections, memorable messaging, differentiation, and simplification of complex ideas. When used effectively, these three pillars work together to create resonant, compelling, and impactful communications that capture the attention and loyalty of the target audience.

Author(s) bio

Ramesh Vemuganti is a renowned speaker and leadership coach with over 40 years of experience in sales and management. He holds a bachelor's degree in Electrical and Communications Engineering and an MBA in Marketing. As a skilled sales motivational trainer, Vemuganti has delivered over 3,000 lectures to hundreds of thousands of students, professionals, and faculty members.

Akshay K. Vemuganti, Ramesh's son, serves as a Business Development Executive based in Seattle. Akshay studied Industrial Engineering, earning degrees from Osmania University and the University of Southern California. He has gained extensive business AI, and entrepreneurial experience across Fortune 500 firms and startups over the past 15 years.

Together, Ramesh's wealth of experience and Akshay's cutting-edge expertise represent a powerful synergy, positioning this father-son duo as valuable coaches for aspiring leaders and entrepreneurs seeking guidance to win the business landscape.

www.ingramcontent.com/pod-product-compliance
Lightning Source LLC
LaVergne TN
LVHW070259170826
845679LV00030B/1498

9798896106166